Quarter Horses

by Grace Hansen

abdopublishing.com

Published by Abdo Kids, a division of ABDO, P.O. Box 398166, Minneapolis, Minnesota 55439.

Copyright © 2017 by Abdo Consulting Group, Inc. International copyrights reserved in all countries. No part of this book may be reproduced in any form without written permission from the publisher.

Printed in the United States of America, North Mankato, Minnesota.

102016

012017

 THIS BOOK CONTAINS RECYCLED MATERIALS

Photo Credits: Alamy, iStock, Shutterstock

Production Contributors: Teddy Borth, Jennie Forsberg, Grace Hansen

Design Contributors: Dorothy Toth, Laura Mitchell

Publisher's Cataloging in Publication Data

Names: Hansen, Grace, author.

Title: Quarter horses / by Grace Hansen.

Description: Minneapolis, Minnesota : Abdo Kids, 2017 | Series: Horses | Includes bibliographical references and index.

Identifiers: LCCN 2016944104 | ISBN 9781680809299 (lib. bdg.) | ISBN 9781680796391 (ebook) | ISBN 9781680797060 (Read-to-me ebook)

Subjects: LCSH: Quarter horses--Juvenile literature.

Classification: DDC 636.1/33--dc23

LC record available at http://lccn.loc.gov/2016944104

Table of Contents

Quarter Horses

The quarter horse is a very popular **breed**. It is for good reason! The breed is smart, quick, and kind.

5

The quarter horse is one of the oldest known **breeds**. It was first bred in the 1660s. It is a cross between Spanish and English horses.

This horse got its name for how fast it can run a quarter mile. Thoroughbreds soon outshined them in racing. But quarters found their place as **stock horses**.

9

The quarter horse is short and sturdy. It has powerful **hindquarters**. This makes it **nimble**.

A quarter horse's head and neck are short. Its neck is also muscular.

13

The quarter horse comes in many colors. Common colors include **bay**, brown, and black.

15

Uses & Personality

Quarter horses are calm
and kind. They are also
very smart. This has made
them a widely loved breed.

16

Early cowboys saw the potential in this horse. Quarter horses have great **agility**. They also work naturally with cattle.

Today's quarter horses have many talents. They are trained in jumping, rodeo, and racing. They can even hunt or play polo.

21

More Facts

- Quarter horses are very calm. This makes them great for people young and old who want to learn to ride.

- In racing, Quarter horses are quick out of the gate. They can run nearly 50 mph (80.5 km/h). They tire after about a quarter mile.

- Quarter horses do very well in cattle roping, team roping, and barrel racing events.

Glossary

agility – the power of moving quickly and easily.

bay – reddish brown.

breed – a certain kind of horse.

hindquarters – the rear part of an animal.

nimble – quick and light in movement.

stock horse – a horse that is trained to herd livestock.

23

Index

abdokids.com

Use this code to log on to abdokids.com and access crafts, games, videos and more!

Abdo Kids Code:
HQK9299